# With
# Gratitude

## The Power of a
## Thank You Note

by
Jennifer Richwine

Produced and Distributed By:

Wake Forest University Digital Publishing

1834 Wake Forest Road

Winston-Salem, North Carolina 27109

http://digitalpublishing.wfu.edu

ISBN 978-1-50322-046-1

# Acknowledgements

*The author would like to thank...*

**Marty and Betty Richwine (Mom and Dad)** for
teaching me how powerful a thank you can be.

**Darnell Hines, Lawson Drinkard, Mark Petersen,
and Lynne Wester** for being the first to tell me there
was "something" to my passion for thank you notes,
and for giving me my first opportunities to take it on
the road.

**Laine Conway, Amy Carlan, Betsy Chapman,
Allison McWilliams, Holly Battle, JoAnn Peroutka,
and Lawson Drinkard** for being most excellent
readers and critiquing my first draft with keen eyes
and insight.

**Laine Conway** for market research, articles galore,
and general all-round cheerleading.

**Cheryl Fischer, Elliot Berke and Scott Carpenter and Mary Tribble** for reading the initial outline and encouraging me to take it one step further.

**Bill Kane** for being an incredibly funny, encouraging and wise guide and mentor throughout the entire process.

**Ken Bennett** for capturing so beautifully my personal thank you cards for the cover photo.

**Katherine and Steve Thomas**s for the loan of the perfect Maine writing hideaway.

**My Ardmore neighbor-friends and First Presbyterian Church family** in Winston-Salem, NC for giving me so many reasons to be thankful, grateful and happy these last fifteen years.

*Thank you all very much!*

# Contents

Acknowledgements          v

Introduction          1

101 Reasons Thank You Notes
are Important          7

Going Beyond the Gift – Good Times
to Write Thank You Notes          31

Taking it to the Next Level – Making
Thank You Notes Creative
and Meaningful          49

Good Habits Die Hard – Making
a Difference One Thank You
Note at a Time          79

About the Author          87

# Introduction

 *"Silent gratitude isn't much use to anyone."*
— *G.B. Stern*

Thank you notes were non-negotiable in my house growing up. My mother was a stickler on writing thank you notes when we received gifts for birthdays or holidays, and often we weren't even allowed to enjoy the gift until the thank you note was written, stamped, and in the mail. Like most children, I balked at the idea and hated trying to come up with the right thing to say. As I moved through high school and college, when my mother did not

1

influence as much control over me, I continued writing thank you notes because I knew it was the right thing to do, even when I hated every second of it.

As I moved into my first job, my first apartment and my first time truly on my own, I became more disconnected from the people who had always been so prevalent in my life. I realized how much I missed these friends and family and wondered if they understood just how important they were to me. So one Thanksgiving, I decided to make a list of the people who had been important influences in my life over the past year, and I proceeded to write thank you notes to every single person on that list, thanking them for a kindness, a friendship, a piece of well-timed advice. And as I wrote, I began to feel overwhelming gratitude for all of these people I had in my life. I never realized just how fortunate I was until I actually put into words why I was thankful for them.

As the notes began arriving in mailboxes, my phone started ringing. Friends and colleagues and family were delighted and surprised, thankful themselves, to receive my notes of thanksgiving. Common phrases were "I didn't know it meant so much to you," or "I can't believe you took the time to write that," or "I've never been thanked for just being me before." It quickly became clear to me that something special was happening, simply because I had taken the time to say (write) thank you. I also recalled my mother's long-forgotten words when I would tell her something nice that someone had done for me: "Don't tell me," she would say. "You need to say these things to them ... how will they ever know if you don't?" How right she was.

Over the next five years, I continued making a list throughout the year, and at Thanksgiving I would sit down and write twenty, fifty, sometimes seventy-five thank you notes to the people in my life who had given me reasons to feel, and BE, thankful. People told me it was one of their favorite things all year and that they looked forward to it because it reminded them of how important a simple note of thanks really is.

I don't write notes at Thanksgiving anymore. I write them all year, every week, sometimes every day. I've found that there's no point in waiting to tell someone how much you appreciate them, and there is much to be gained by doing it now. I write notes to colleagues, friends, family, people I meet when I travel, hotel staff, the guy who fixes my car, and anyone else who does something that makes my life easier, makes it fun, makes it special, or brings a smile to my face. Because that matters. And although it may sound like a cliché, the act of writing thank you notes has changed my life and relationships.

Over the years I've found that often I am the happiest and feel the most gratitude when I'm writing thank you notes. The very act of writing a note of thanks invests me with a renewed sense that I have a pretty good life and many reasons (and people) for which to be grateful. And once I figured this out, I wanted others to benefit from it as well. So a few years ago I put together a short talk about the art and the power of thank you notes. I presented that talk to several groups and departments where I work, and I was blown away by the positive reaction and feedback. Colleagues continued to follow up with me to tell me how their own thank you notes, written after hearing my talk, had impacted their lives and those of their loved ones. I was asked to present at a conference for university stewardship and donor relations professionals, and once again, the feedback reaffirmed what I already knew ... thank you notes are powerful. They are one of the easiest and most positive ways to transform an individual's view of his/her world, as well as impact the life of the receiver. There are so many examples of how a simple note of thanks has transformed a relationship, healed a hurt, bonded individuals who were estranged, or even saved a life.

My college roommate recently pointed out to me that only a small percentage of the population will be able to write timely, creative thank you notes every time someone does something nice for them. She is absolutely correct, and I know that writing thank you notes does not come naturally to everyone. My hope is that this book will give real examples of how to make this an easy, common practice that becomes a joy instead of a burden, a habit instead of a chore, an artful and meaningful endeavor, instead of a lost art. And when it does, I know those who write, and those who receive, will be transformed by this very simple act.

# 101 Reasons Thank You Notes are Important

**(okay... 5 very good reasons)**

## Because it's the right thing to do

 *"The roots of all goodness lie in the soil of appreciation for goodness."*
— *the Dalai Lama*

Just a few days ago, a colleague invited a mutual friend and me over for a middle-of-the-week lunch at his home. We had not all been together in months, even though we had talked about it quite a bit over Facebook and email.

He picked me up at my office and drove me to his new house, then gave me the grand tour that ended in his bright, sunny kitchen where the three of us had a simple lunch of chicken salad, fruit, and homemade cookies. After lunch was over, we moved out to the pool and chatted about life and work and movies with our feet in the cool water and our faces turned towards the sun.

Later that afternoon, our mutual friend texted both of us to tell us how much fun it was to be together. Then she said "I know Jennifer will undoubtedly write you a heartfelt and well-written thank you note and I know that I should but I will never get around to it." My response? "Mine is already in the mail."

Even when we know that we should, we often don't take the time to write thank you notes for kindnesses rendered. And this book is not about adding guilt or undue burden to already hectic and busy lives. It's about showing not only how powerful thank you notes can be, but also how to make writing them as effortless as possible. I wrote my note in the first five minutes of returning to my office. A collection of blank notes was in a prime spot on my desk, and before I checked email or voice mail or popped into a colleague's office to see how the morning meeting went, I sat down to write the note. I wanted my friend to know that his kindness did not go unappreciated, and that not only did I love receiving his invitation to lunch, I also enjoyed the time together immensely. It was a bright spot in my day, and I had looked forward to it all week. And I wanted him to know that and to understand that his efforts to connect were not in vain.

Sometimes we get caught up in the notion that things are "owed" to us – that people should be kind to us and that we deserve this at every turn. The reality, however, is that no one *owes* us anything. When someone steps out of the box of what they "have to do" in order to do something nice for you ... well ... you should tell them it was appreciated. It's as simple as that.

Almost inevitably when I talk about this concept, people will say "I know that I should, but I just don't have the time," or "I get distracted by other things," or "I'm just not disciplined enough to write notes." I get it. We are a busy society. We struggle to find time to cross off even the most basic tasks on our to-do lists. That's why it's especially important to find time to thank those people who do nice things, because they are busy too.

No matter what someone did for you, I will venture a guess that it took more of their time to do what they did than it will for you to write them a note. Did they buy you a gift? Then they had to think of what you might like, shop for the gift (in a store or online), wrap it perhaps, etc. Did they bring you a meal after surgery? Think of the time it took them to grocery shop and prepare the meal. Even if they brought a prepared meal, they made the effort to purchase it and bring it to your house. Did they give you advice on how to deal with a difficult colleague or other work situation? Was the conversation longer than 10 minutes? For any of these situations, the time the person gave you is still infinitely more than the time it should take you to write them a note of gratitude. So there really is no excuse to not taking that time, even precious time in a busy schedule, to say thank you.

If that isn't convincing, I can list a number of *really busy* people who still find the time to write thank you notes. George H. W. Bush is well known for his countless thank you notes, even sometimes writing a note in response to one he had received. Jack Welch, former CEO of GE was an avid note writer to employees for even the smallest achievement or gesture, and Douglas

Conant, the former CEO of the Campbell Soup Company, wrote at least 30,000 thank you notes to employees during his 10 years as head of the large corporation. Facebook's Mark Zuckerberg challenged himself to write a thank you note every day in 2014.

In my fifteen years of working for Wake Forest University, I've received thank you notes from a host of speakers, including Joe Biden, Condoleezza Rice, Michelle Obama, and Colin Powell. These leaders likely have less time on their hands than the average person to write these notes, and I know it is very likely that someone writes these letters for them. The key is that they obviously understand the power of words of gratitude for someone who has done something good and they believe in it enough to make sure they have people who can make this happen.

## They convey simple (and not-so-simple) appreciation

 *"I would maintain that thanks are the highest form of thought, and that gratitude is happiness doubled by wonder."*
—*G.K. Chesterton*

Most people, even if they don't regularly write thank you notes, understand that they are often written to show appreciation for some gesture, large or small. We know that some form of thank you is expected for gifts, hosting, meals prepared, recommendation letters written, advice given, and many other acts of kindness. I really do believe that writing notes for all of these reasons is a good practice and one that should become a habit, part of our weekly or even daily routine. I also think when we only write thank you notes for these simple acts, we miss a huge opportunity to show our appreciation for the greater and more meaningful ways that people influence our lives on a daily basis. These thank you notes can be the most powerful kind – the kind that tell someone that who they are and what they do matters.

When I speak to groups about the power of thank you notes, I usually ask them at the end of the talk to write a note to someone, not for a gift or a recent act of kindness, but for being a special person in their lives in some way. And it doesn't need to be recent – it can be to someone they knew years in the past but who positively affected their life. I ask them to think about teachers, relatives, coaches, old friends or colleagues. I watch them as they begin to conjure up individuals, and inevitably there are smiles on their faces as they remember these special people who made a difference in their lives. Often members of the audience will tell me later that they had forgotten all about this person until that moment, but that it brought back such great memories.

After each of these talks, I always get feedback from those who actually mailed their notes of gratitude. It's possible they didn't receive anything in return from the person they wrote, but they say that through the process of writing they were reminded of how special that person was to them, and how grateful they were to have someone like that in their life at some point in time. Others send me emails and letters to tell me that they received a phone call, text, email, or note from their recipient who was amazed to hear from them, thrilled to know that they had positively influenced their life.

Recently I heard from an employee of the Morehead Planetarium and Science Center in North Carolina. She had attended one of my talks and decided to write to her first boss from thirteen years earlier. After receiving her note of thanks, her former boss called her to say that it came at just the right time, and "it made me sit back in my chair and say 'so this is why I've been put here on Earth.'" The words we write really do matter, and sometimes a note from someone out of the blue can drastically change our mood, our self-confidence, or even our perspective on life. If you've ever received one of these notes, you know just how significant it can be. It's a priceless gift to say to someone "who you are and what you've done matters."

One thing that always surprises me in conversations is the number of people who have never written a thank you note to their closest friends and family members. What I always hear is "they know how I feel about them – they don't need a note." We often think that of course these people know we are grateful for their presence in our lives. *Of course they know*. If you learn nothing else from this book, please learn this: **they don't know unless you tell them!** They just don't. Assuming that they do can cause misunderstanding, miscommunication, and hurt. Writing the note, saying the words, can be more powerful in your relationships than almost anything else.

The summer between my junior and senior year in college, I had an internship in Washington, D.C. and lived with my aunt and her family.

That summer I spent a lot of time reflecting on my college experience and my life up to that point. Towards the end of the summer, I had planned to write my parents to thank them for the college education I had received due to their hard work and many years of saving almost every penny they earned so that I would graduate without debt. As I sat down to write this letter, I began to contemplate my life and how fortunate I was to have parents who loved me so much and had taught me so many wonderful lessons in life. So instead of writing one letter, I wrote two, one to each of them. In addition to saying thank you for my college experience, I focused on very specific things that made each of them such special parents and used real examples of things they had done to influence my life in a positive way.

A few days after mailing these letters, my mother called me from home on her lunch break, weeping into the phone. I was a bit stunned and asked my mother why she was crying. "You know how I feel about you," I said. "This can't be a surprise." And my mother responded with words I will never forget. "I always knew that you loved me," she said. "I just didn't know that you thought I was a good mother." Oh ... my ... goodness. Had I really never said these words to her before?

How was this possible? And yet, in that moment, I shamefully realized that it was true. I had thought it many times, had given thanks to God for each of my parents on countless occasions, but I had never told *them*. My mother keeps this letter in her Bible and has brought it up in conversations many times over the years because it means so much to her.

It was a stunning reminder to me that those closest to us really don't know how we feel unless we tell them. A letter is a way to say those precious words so our loved ones can keep them forever in their possession. We need to write to our spouse, our partner, our kids, our siblings, our best friends, and let them know just why they are so special to us. It's a gift that costs nothing but means the world to them. A friend of mine recently wrote to her thirteen year old daughter and told her about the many special qualities she admired in her. She had noticed that her daughter was getting caught up in a teenage girl's normal angst about her looks, grades, and social status, and my friend wanted her daughter to understand how much she loved her beyond any of these things. So she wrote a note that thanked her for being kind to their elderly neighbor, for being generous to her siblings, and for being a gracious loser when her team suffered a defeat on the field. This letter, my friend said, gave her daughter a boost of confidence that changed how she saw herself, so much so that my friend wondered why she hadn't thought to write those words to her daughter sooner.

We have all had people we love leave this world too soon, and many of us have experienced the devastation of not having a chance to tell a loved one just how we felt about them. That's why I tell anyone who will listen to write those letters. Tell those closest to you how you feel about them so that they can enjoy that NOW. It will make all the difference in the world to them, and you will never have to wonder if you waited too long to say the things that needed to be said.

## They remind us of the many reasons we have to be grateful

 *"Give thanks for a little and you will find a lot."*
*—Hansa Proverb*

It never fails. Every time I've completed a thank you note, I find myself even more grateful for the person I'm writing to than I was before I started. Writing notes to anyone for any act of kindness fills me up with thoughts of gratitude for the things I have in my life, even when I'm not feeling very grateful. Many times I feel anything but thankful, but I still sit down to write the notes on my list, often with a frustrated sense of obligation. And once I've crossed a few notes off my list, I am reminded again that my life is pretty good. Just putting into words what someone's generosity, or patience, or wisdom means to you makes it impossible to ignore that those are gifts you receive, sometimes even when you don't deserve them.

Several years ago a colleague who knew my passion for thank you notes asked if I had read *365 Thank Yous: The Year a Simple Act of Daily Gratitude Changed My Life* by John Kralik. I was surprised that I had not heard about it before and immediately ordered it. I read the book in one sitting and now recommend it to everyone I talk to about thank you notes. Kralik's story is a perfect example of how the discipline of writing notes of gratitude can actually make someone grateful when they weren't before. The book begins at a very low point in Kralik's life – he was painfully making his way through a second divorce, his law firm was suffering, he was estranged from his children, he was overweight, out of shape and depressed. One New Year's Day he decided to go on a hike, where he inexplicably felt moved to focus the next year of his life on gratitude. There on a mountain Kralik decided he would write 365 thank you notes over the next year. For a man who was losing all of the things that were important to him, who had little, it seemed, for which to be grateful, this was a bold and surprising resolution. It turns out that it immeasurably changed his life for the good.

Kralik did not always find it easy to write notes, and there were times when he wondered if he would really make his goal of 365 in a year. But he continued to look for reasons to write notes to people and found that when he was actually seeking reasons to feel thankful, he found them at every turn. After a friend and fellow attorney spent over an hour on the phone giving him advice, Kralik writes "It was only because I was searching for a reason to write a thank-you note each day that I realized I should be more than just a little thankful for a friend like this." And after writing a note to a Starbucks employee to thank him for always greeting him warmly and remembering his name, he was astonished at how much a note like this meant to the recipient. "And he taught me a lesson," Kralik writes, "that there is value in the smallest notes, and in being thankful for what seems like the smallest thing."

As I read his book, it occurred to me that what Kralik was doing during that year was writing a gratitude journal in the form of thank you notes. Read most any self-help book or magazine article on the subject of gratitude or happiness or fighting depression, and they will all tell you that keeping a gratitude journal leads to feelings of genuine happiness. I've heard from countless friends and acquaintances who say that when they are diligent about keeping a gratitude journal, they spend their days looking for even the smallest reasons to be thankful, and that it changes their outlook on their life. I've never kept a gratitude journal. I've never really felt the need to do so, and I think it's because this habit of writing notes on a regular basis is my own form of a journal, with the added benefit that the people in my life for whom I'm grateful actually know it. I love the idea of a gratitude journal, but even more I love the idea of turning these grateful thoughts into notes, like Kralik's, which inspire others to be more grateful as well. When you fill your head and your heart with this kind of gratitude, there simply isn't room for anything negative.

## They strengthen your relationships

 *"In ordinary life, we hardly realize that we receive a great deal more than we give, and that it is only with gratitude that life becomes rich."*
—Dietrich Bonhoeffer

Several years ago, I was stumped at work by a colleague with whom I just couldn't connect. She and I did not see eye to eye on a number of issues, and often I suspected she might be going behind my back to try to win others over to her side on key decisions. My colleague was higher in the organization than I was, and I didn't feel like I was at a place in my career where I could address the issue head-on with her. After several months of complaining about my situation to a friend, he asked me "Is there anything you like about this person? Anything at all?" After a few minutes, I rattled off some areas where this colleague really excelled, and I knew that these were things no one else at the office could do so they were pretty important to our success. So

I decided to take my own advice and write her a note to tell her how much I appreciated the skill set she had, and how it really seemed to make certain things run smoother in the office. I didn't exaggerate those skills, and I wasn't insincere or sappy in my thanks. It was a short note that simply stated my appreciation for her work. After my colleague received the note, she came into my office to thank me, in person, for words that she said she needed to hear. In the years since then, our working relationship hasn't been perfect, but we both try to see the good in each other, and I've received several notes from her as well.

I think the note was a powerful way to show her that I really did appreciate her work and the ways she positived contributed to our office, but I also needed to write the note to remind myself that she wasn't all bad, and that our relationship wasn't black and white. Everyone has gifts and positive things we can appreciate, but when we get bogged down in the things that drive us crazy, we can't see the good that is there as well. This can especially be true for spouses, siblings, children, in-laws and anyone who is closest to us. So often we mire ourselves in all of the ways people disappoint us or hurt us, even to the point we can no longer recognize the things they do that make us happy. Picking out one thing for which to say thanks, then writing it in a note, can make all the difference in the way they see themselves *and* in the way you feel about them.

The Ben Franklin Effect is a psychological finding that says "A person who has done someone a favor is more likely to do that person another favor than they would be if they had received a favor from that person." It's named after Ben Franklin after he observed this very thing in his own work and wrote about it in his autobiography. About a rival legislator he said "Having heard that he had in his library a certain very scarce and curious book, I wrote a note to him, expressing my desire of perusing that book, and requesting he would do me the favour of lending it to me for a few days. He sent it immediately, and I return'd it in about a week with another note, expressing strongly my sense of the favour. When we next met in the House, he spoke to me (which he had never done before), and with great civility; and he ever manifested a readiness to serve me on all occasions, so that we became great friends, and our friendship continued to his death." Both favors and notes of gratitude enrich and enhance our relationships.

I've noticed the Ben Franklin Effect not just with adversaries or those with whom we don't connect, but also with our closest friends, family, and colleagues. Study after study has shown that we are attracted to people who make us feel good about ourselves and those we think actually like us. It makes sense, then, that when you make a habit of writing notes of thanks to those around you, those individuals will naturally gravitate to you. It affirms their positive feelings and the value of the relationship.

Many of my closest friends live far away, and it isn't often we are able to spend time together. They have busy lives with their children, work, and volunteer activities, and it's rare we can even spend a few minutes chatting on the phone. While my life is busy as well, I am not married and don't have kids, so my time is at least a little more flexible, and often I sense my friends feel guilty about not having as much time to spend together as we both would like. So when we do get a quick phone call in, or an unexpected visit over a long weekend, I always write them a note of thanks, to say that I'm glad we are the kind of friends that can always pick up wherever we left off, and how wonderful it is to have a friendship that isn't diminished by miles or months between visits. I do this because I want my friends to know how much I appreciate them in any circumstance, and I want them to think of our friendship with happiness instead of guilt. At the risk of sounding like a broken record, writing thank you notes is a simple, quick and inexpensive way to bolster a relationship, good or bad, for the better.

## They give you a competitive advantage (and yes, it's okay if that's your motivation)

 *"The thankful receiver bears a plentiful harvest."*
—*William Blake*

It is extraordinarily rare for someone to tell me they don't think that writing thank you notes is important. In almost every conversation I have about this topic, everyone agrees that it's a good thing to do, that is shouldn't be a lost art, that it's not old fashioned, but a habit that has sadly gone by the wayside. And yet, so few people I talk to actually make it a regular part of their routine. If I had to put a purely non-scientific, anecdotal number on it, I'd say less than 30% of the people I ask write thank you notes on a regular basis, and many people tell me they can't even remember the last time they actually wrote a note. Yet when I ask the same people if they can recall a thank you note they received that was special to them, they all have stories of a note that came at just the right time, said something that changed their outlook, or just made them happy for the entire day after reading it. So many people believe in the power and the goodness of thank you notes, but few actually follow through with writing them.

For this reason, writing thank you notes makes you different, it makes you stand out, and it gives you an advantage in what is often a competitive marketplace. Just spend five minutes researching this topic on the Internet, and you will find quote after quote from business executives and CEOs who say that in today's society of emails with phrases instead of sentences, texts filled with abbreviated words, and tweets with 140 characters or less, a handwritten note (more on the handwritten part later) really sets someone apart in the professional world. One CEO stated "Those who take the time to send a note of thanks go into my mental list of people I will continue to remember and look out for. My colleagues have said the same. The authors of the five notes I have sitting on my desk remain at the top of my mind when I hear of job or internship openings." Another executive said "I've hired hundreds of people, and the handwritten notes always win out, and there's not one exception. Handwritten notes stand out. Handwritten notes take a whole lot more thought and effort."

Working on a college campus, I have many opportunities to talk with students about a variety of things, but most often they are interested in talking with me about my career path and advice I might have for them when looking for internships or jobs. I always, always encourage them to write notes to those who interview them or just take the time out of their schedule to give them advice. While some interviewers and professionals don't expect a note, receiving one still makes the writer stand out in their mind, whether it's for the job at hand or one down the road.

In a May 2014 issue of *Entrepreneur*, author, etiquette expert and founder of The Protocol School of Palm Beach, Jacqueline Whitmore, says "Thank you notes may seem like a habit of an older generation, but at my company I encourage more and more professionals to make it a part of their weekly routine. The benefits are well worth the investment of time and energy. Thank you notes can help you make new connections, grow relationships, and show your thoughtfulness."

I write notes to colleagues inside and outside my organization who I think someday I might want to work with or partner with on a project. I don't write things I don't genuinely mean, and I don't make up reasons to thank them, but when I see something I appreciate, I let them know. Writing those notes will strengthen our relationship and likely increase the potential for future possibilities down the road. Is it calculated? Maybe a little. But the reality is that it works. Taking the time to write notes now can plant the seeds for positive things in the future that you haven't even imagined.

Ben C. Sutton, Jr., Chairman and President of IMG College (a division of WME/IMG, the world's leading sports, entertainment and talent agency), is a big believer in thank you notes and for over two decades has incorporated them into his business. Every Friday morning, members of his 1,000-person team are asked to invest thirty minutes to compose thank you notes to partners, sponsors, colleagues and even vendors. In fact, part of the new employee on-boarding welcome package is personalized notecards.

When I asked Sutton why he was so devoted to the practice of writing thank you notes and invested so much time and energy instilling this discipline within the organization, he told me that hands-down it is one of the most important things the company does to distinguish itself in a highly competitive industry. "If you ask me to point to three or four of the most important cultural attributes or points of distinction for us in a space where we compete daily with the NFL and ESPN, one of those would be *making* the time to express our gratitude to others in an extraordinarily and unfortunately, increasingly unique way – take 5 minutes to make it permanent by penning a note!"

Sutton has the younger staff in his office on board with the practice as well. "Many of them have never written a note of any kind to someone else in their own handwriting. So they may do it at first because they think they should – but then they see how their professional and personal relationships are enhanced by it. They receive great feedback and begin writing notes on their own time, because they see the results it brings." Sutton says in a fast-paced, ultra-competitive business, thank you notes are the distinctive outlier that sets him and his team apart from the rest.

# Going Beyond the Gift – Good Times to Write Thank You Notes

I'm not going to insult anyone by spending too much time on the obvious situations – yes, you should always write thank you notes when:

➢ someone gives you a gift
➢ when you are a guest in someone's home
➢ when someone does you a favor that was above and beyond the normal call of duty
➢ when someone writes you a job recommendation
➢ after an interview for a job or internship

31

These are pretty much givens, and they don't bear as much explanation as the ones below. The following situations are often overlooked and become missed opportunities to convey gratitude.

## When someone gives you their advice or time

 *"How beautiful a day can be when kindness touches it!"*
—*George Elliston*

I am always amazed at how few job-seekers and students follow up with a thank you note after I've sat down to talk to them, at their request, to give them advice. Often my days are filled with meetings and events, sometimes back-to-back. Countless days I eat at my desk just to catch up on emails. It's not a practice I would recommend and a habit I'm trying hard to break, but with a packed day sometimes you have to make choices. So when I've given an hour of a very busy day, it's not with the expectation that I will receive a thank you note afterwards, but I always feel much better about how that time was spent when I receive a thank you note.

I don't know anyone today who doesn't feel crunched for time, pressed every day with commitments to work, family, volunteer work, social obligations, exercise, etc. Every single one of my colleagues and friends looks for more hours in the day because there just aren't enough to get everything done. Time is a precious, precious commodity, and when someone volunteers to give some of their time in order to help you in some way, it's important to acknowledge that. Doing so can only strengthen your relationship with that person – they will remember your note and are likely to be more open to future conversations.

A number of years ago, towards the end of the exam week in spring semester, I ran into a graduating senior I had gotten to know through a president's aides program. I was running errands on the main part of campus to get ready for an upcoming event, but I didn't want to miss the opportunity to say hello to him since he would soon be leaving campus for good. When I asked him how things were going and what he was planning to do after graduation, his face fell and he said he was struggling between two job opportunities and while he was grateful to have not one, but two options, he was paralyzed with the choice and didn't know how he was going to make a decision. I asked if he wanted to chat about it over coffee and he immediately said yes. We spent the next hour or so talking about the options, the pros and cons, and what he needed to know about himself and about the very different job opportunities in order to make a decision. I'm not a career counselor, and I've certainly made some mistakes in my own career, but it was obvious he needed a voice he trusted to help him think things through.

Less than forty-eight hours later, I had an email from the student. He first apologized that he wasn't sending me a handwritten note, but explained that he was literally moving out of his residence hall and had already packed up everything he owned, including pens and paper. But he didn't want to leave without first telling me how much he appreciated our conversation ... he mentioned that he knew I was busy (in fact, I was planning his upcoming graduation) and for that reason he was very grateful that I had taken the time to meet with him, especially on the spur of the moment. I was thrilled with his email and knew he was well on his way to being successful in whatever industry he chose, in part because he already understood that time is a gift, and he inherently got the importance of being gracious and grateful to anyone willing to give that to him. Several years ago, I ran into him on the streets of Washington, D.C. He was in town just briefly before he returned to his job overseas. It was no surprise to me that he had been very successful in the few short years since he graduated and he reinforced this when he thanked me yet again for the time I had given him on that stressful day of exam week. I told him how much the note had meant and encouraged him to keep on writing those ... and I'm pretty sure he does.

## When someone is just "doing their job"

 *"God gave you 86,400 seconds today. Have you used one to say thank you?"*
—*William Arthur Ward*

For fifteen years, I planned events for Wake Forest University. One of the things I loved about my job was that I received a lot of feedback, good and bad, for the work that I did. The events I planned were high profile, so a lot of people saw on a regular basis the fruits of my labor, and it wasn't atypical to receive notes of gratitude from colleagues, faculty, donors, and trustees after a major event on campus. I loved getting these notes and knowing that my work was appreciated, and I had many opportunities to reflect on what I did and how my work helped move the university forward. But the notes that meant the most to me over the years were the ones that arrived not after a large gala or graduation ceremony, but at the most unexpected of times.

One note that sticks in my mind came from a trustee who had served the university for a number of years. She wrote a note to me that she included with a registration form for an upcoming event, and she thanked me for "always taking such good care of me and all of the trustees." She noted that I always greeted them with a smile on my face and looked for ways to make their lives easier when they were visiting campus. "You are perfect at what you do," she said, "and we at Wake Forest are lucky to have you." It's one of the notes that I treasure the most, because I'm not sure what prompted it, and it was wholly unexpected but served to remind me why I was in that role and how my work, even when I wasn't consciously aware of it, made a difference to others.

There are many jobs and careers where the work is not as easy to see or recognize on a regular basis. Many people, day in and day out, work quietly and diligently at their jobs, jobs that make a big difference, but aren't recognized for the important role that they play in their organization. Often employees are only noticed when something doesn't go well, even though the things that they do right far outweigh one mistake or one bad day. When I speak to people about thank you notes, especially in corporate or professional settings, I always talk about the need to thank people just for doing their jobs. It is an amazing and inexpensive way to boost morale for an organization or an individual. In my department, there is an external group that is constantly interacting with alumni, donors, and constituents, and then there is another group that works behind the scenes to make sure everything runs smoothly – they are the ones who keep our computers up and running, the ones who keep our database accurate and up to date, the ones who help us run reports and lists for invitations, the ones who record gifts and send letters of acknowledgment to donors. Without these people, many of us wouldn't be able to do our jobs, yet it's rare that they are thanked for their work ... for just doing their job.

It doesn't take much to acknowledge someone's work. Last spring I met with some of our data and reporting staff about some invitation lists that I needed for an upcoming event. I needed the lists to include a lot of information that I didn't know how to retrieve, and it was a complicated process I didn't understand. The team members gave me over an hour of their time to really figure out what it was that I wanted to do and to make sure they understood the purpose behind what I was doing so they could provide me with the best information to help me accomplish my goal. Afterwards, I was so grateful for their attention to detail, their desire not to just check something off their list, but to really help make my job easier. I wrote them all notes and thanked them for ... yes ... doing their job ... but doing it in a way that gave me a better sense of teamwork and collaboration. It was obvious that they took pride in their work, and it was important to take notice of this and let them know that it was appreciated.

This is equally important for those working in the service industry, who often only hear complaints and rarely are thanked for the things that go well. The Starbucks barista mentioned in John Kralik's book is a perfect example. The employee was shocked by Kralik's note, in large part because he was so used to hearing complaints. When Kralik thanked him for doing exactly what Starbucks employees are trained to do, he was astonished. I've made it a habit to write notes to those service employees who really do make my life better, even in the smallest way. I've written notes to car mechanics, hotel staff, waitresses, drive-thru window workers at the dry cleaners, and yes, Starbucks baristas. It's not uncommon for these people to say that it's the only note they've ever received for just "doing my job," but they always follow that up to say that it meant the world to them and it gave them a deeper feeling of pride in their work.

 *"None of us got to where we are alone. Whether the assistance we received was obvious or subtle, acknowledging some-one's help is a big part of understanding the importance of saying thank you."*
—*Harvey Mackay*

A few years ago at Wake Forest University, at a required meeting for graduating seniors, the student body president, who was obviously a big fan of thank you notes as well, asked everyone to think about those who had influenced their lives in a positive way during their four years of college – people who had given them their time for any number of reasons. She prodded them to think not just about faculty and administrators, but the people who managed the intramural sports teams, the librarian who helped them with research materials in the wee hours of the night, the cafeteria worker who always fixed their taco salad just like they wanted it, or the facilities crew member who shoveled snow at 5:30 a.m. so they could get safely to where they needed to go on campus. She gently reminded the seniors that though many of them had paid full tuition to be there, the many people who had helped them along the way during the past four years deserved to be thanked, especially since many of them worked for hourly wages and had some of the most difficult, often thankless jobs on campus. Then she asked each senior to write notes to five individuals on campus to tell them that they had made a difference in their lives at Wake Forest. She was resourceful and had worked with a local printer who donated over 5,000 thank you notes for the students to use. She had ordered extra so she also encouraged the seniors to take more than five if they had more people to thank.

I loved witnessing that moment. I loved that a twenty-one year old student had already learned how important it is to thank the people around you, ordinary people doing ordinary things that make an extraordinary difference in our lives. I'm sure not every senior fulfilled the student body president's request. In fact, I would be surprised if even half of them wrote thank you notes before graduation. But she planted a seed in their minds, and even if only twenty-five seniors wrote five notes each, there are 125 people who received notes of gratitude. I'm guessing for those 125, the notes made their day and reminded them why they do their jobs.

## When you think maybe you should

 *"We can only be said to be alive in those moments when our hearts are conscious of our treasures."*
*—Thornton Wilder*

There is only one way to say this ... if you think maybe you should write someone a thank you note, then you should! If it enters your mind that someone is deserving of thanks, then write that name down on a piece of paper and promise yourself you will write them a note ... and then do it! I'm always surprised when people tell me they "thought about writing" me a note, but then didn't. I'm not sure what message they think they are sending by telling me this, but I always think to myself "I guess what I did wasn't really that important." After one of my presentations on thank you notes, a man in his forties wrote to me to say that over the years he had "written many, many thank you notes in my head, but they have never seen paper." While I was glad that the purpose of his note was to tell me that my talk had inspired him to make a habit out of writing thank you notes, it also made me sad to think of the people who had missed out on his expression of gratitude, and the words that might have been exactly the affirmation they needed at the time.

I'm a big believer in intuition, so I tell people they should always write notes when someone pops in their head that they think they should thank. Even if the note is coming ten years after an act of kindness, it will mean something to the receiver. It may mean even more, to be remembered long after the act itself. I would love to fill up an entire book with examples of notes that came to people at just the right time, with just the right words, because they arrived in a dark hour or month or period of despair. Following are two examples from my own experience that illustrate this – one note that I wrote and another that I received.

In my late twenties I was living in Washington, D.C., and still trying to figure out what I wanted to be when I grew up. I was in a long term relationship with a man twelve years my senior, and most of our conversations began to center on our future ... a future upon which we didn't necessarily agree. We began going to a counselor in Virginia, a small, British man who had a calming force that instantly made me feel comfortable. For months, we met with him once a week, together and separately, to try to figure out if we were going to make it as a couple. After more than six months of counseling, we finally broke up, abruptly, and I moved back to North Carolina to start over with a new direction in life. But before I moved, I met with the counselor several times as he helped me work through my feelings of doubt, insecurity, and inadequacy. He sent me on my way with many good words and things to think about as I moved forward on my new adventure.

In the fall of that year, when I began writing my then annual Thanksgiving notes, I decided to write to the counselor, to tell him how much I appreciated the things he had taught me. I pointed to some specific things he had said that had helped me, and I gave him updates on some areas he had encouraged me to improve. I emphasized how much his advice had helped me at a time that I needed it the most. Then I stamped and mailed the note and never gave it another thought – in fact – it was something I did out of duty as it was cathartic for me to put words to paper that signified I was making progress in my life.

At Christmas time, I received a card from the counselor, with a story inside that brought me to tears. Apparently, earlier that fall the counselor had been struggling with his work. He didn't feel like his clients were making progress and he blamed himself for that. He was tired, weary of the career he had held for over three decades, and yet he wondered what else there was for him to do at this stage of his life. After a particularly unproductive and frustrating session with a client, he had almost convinced himself that it was time to retire from the work that used to bring him such satisfaction, joy and a sense of accomplishment. In the time he had between clients, he decided to take a walk to the post office to try to clear his head and find a more positive outlook on his situation. That was the day he received my note. He sat on a bench and read my words of affirmation and gratitude, words that he had longed to hear but had not for so long, and he was astounded that they had come at just the moment he really needed to hear them. He told me that my note had reminded him that his work had purpose, that he was good at what he did, and that there were people whose lives were better because of him. He thanked me for my note and said that it had renewed in him a sense of peace that he was right where he should be, doing exactly what he should be doing. Never doubt the power of a thank you note to transform a life.

In similar fashion, several years into my new career in North Carolina, I received a note that was equally restorative and affirming. It was one of my more difficult semesters, filled with events that were complicated and time consuming, and we planned them with an under-staffed team, which meant long hours, nights and weekends. I had neglected many of my friendships and relationships and was starting to understand the phrase "married to my job." One late night, after hours of trying to get a banquet seating chart to match up to the registered attendees, I left the office without even turning off my computer or lights, knowing I would return in just a few short hours and resume my frustrated attempts to make things right. The next morning, as I walked in bleary eyed and exhausted, I noticed something sticking out from under my office door. It was a plain white envelope with "Ms. Richwine" written on the front. Inside was a folded piece of white copy paper, with a handwritten note from a student. The first line said "I am writing you this letter to sincerely thank you for all of the work that you do at Wake Forest." And later, "Because you work so hard, often behind the scenes, to make these events possible, I wanted to take the time to thank you. You help make Wake Forest the thriving, desirable place it is today." I sat at my desk and cried, amazed that a student had taken the time to write this to me, at a time when I wondered why I was doing this job and if it made any difference. She assured me that it was, and I will always be grateful for her words that arrived just when I needed them. They gave me the strength to make it through another week of long hours and many events. I will never know what prompted that student to write me that note, but I'm glad that she did. And I'm even more convinced, being on this side of a thank you note, that they are powerful. When you think you should ... do. It could mean the world to the person on the receiving end of your words of gratitude.

## When you need to feel more grateful

 *"It is impossible to feel grateful and depressed in the same moment."*
—*Naomi Williams*

One of the reasons I stopped writing my annual Thanksgiving notes is that I ended up with too many to write at one time. Once you start looking for reasons to say thank you, you will be astounded by the number of people and incidents that come along in a day, a week, a year that warrant a note of thanks. In the beginning, I kept lists throughout the year, but it became too much to do in one short month, and it dawned on me that there was no need for people to wait a month, or six months, to learn of my gratitude. Now I write notes every week, if not every day. I never write a note that is not sincere, and I don't write notes for things that don't make me grateful, but there are enough good people and good deeds in my life to fill up more notes than I will ever be able to write.

Have you ever heard a word that you never knew before, and once you learned it, you started seeing and hearing it everywhere ... on the news, in a magazine, in a sermon or speech ... and you wonder how it is that you never knew this word before? I've found that it's the same with gratitude. If someone asked you right now to list five things that have happened today, or in the past week, that made you thankful, you might have a tough time listing them off quickly. But once the question is out there, and you start looking for your list of five, or ten, or fifteen, you will find them easier and faster than you can imagine.

I do believe, as the quote at the beginning of this section states, that it's impossible to feel grateful and depressed at the same time. A friend challenges me on this sometimes when I am struggling with depression or frustration or anger. She quietly asks me "have you written any thank you notes lately?" She knows that as soon as I write a few thank you notes, my outlook will be more positive, because it forces me to acknowledge the good things in my life. And when I'm grateful, it's almost guaranteed I won't be grumpy, or sulky or sad.

That's why I also make it a practice to write notes to those who make me unhappy, because it forces me to see something good in them that I might not have seen before. Even with those who have hurt or angered me greatly, I always (okay ... almost always) find *something* about them for which to be thankful. Writing that note, while it might force me to be humble and swallow some pride, brings me a sense of peace that I would never have found if I had let myself wallow in negative emotions.

Be vigilant about looking for the good things that are happening around you every day. It's up to you to say thank you.

# Taking it to the Next Level – Making Thank You Notes Creative and Meaningful

*"Hem your blessings with thankfulness so they don't unravel."*
*—Unknown*

I am not an expert in etiquette, and even the masters of protocol have varied, conflicting, and often strong feelings about how thank you notes should be written. There are plenty of formulas for writing the perfect note, and I've read countless articles and books that give very specific instructions on what to include, what never to say, and the five things that must appear in a note. While these are all very helpful and informative, there really is no set way to write a thank you note. I care much more about how effective and meaningful my notes are than if I have followed a tried and true formula. Notes are best when they are unique and personal, for the writer and the receiver. That means that no two of my notes are ever alike.

This section is not to list for you the essential elements (or never do's) of thank you notes, but to give you some thoughts and tips for how to write all of your notes in a way that has a positive impact on the recipient. Even if you feel you "have" to write a thank you note out of obligation or protocol, you might as well compose one that will be remembered.

## Handwrite all of your notes! (or) Handwritten > Typed > Email

This is the part that always makes people groan. No one seems to like to handwrite notes, and no one thinks they have good handwriting which makes the task even less desirable. And now that many elementary schools aren't even teaching cursive to students, I'm guessing this will continue to be a sticking point for thank you notes. However, there is nothing that can come close to the personal touch of a handwritten thank you note. It tells the recipient that it's not a standard note with the obligatory words, it says that you thought enough of them to take the time to write out your feelings for them. And it definitely stands out today amongst all of the bills, junk mail, and emails we get. I know that when I receive an envelope that is addressed to me by hand, I save it to read after I've opened all of the standard junk, because I want to savor it.

Inevitably when I talk to people about handwritten notes, I always get a question about why they can't be typed and/or emailed. My answer ... it's just not the same as a handwritten note. A typed letter feels cold and impersonal, where a handwritten note conveys warmth. The stationery itself for handwritten notes is more personal and distinguishable from a typed letter. Most people know that with a typed letter there is a good chance an administrative assistant typed it, or even worse, composed it. There are certainly CEOs and other leaders who have employees learn to mimic their handwriting so they can write their notes for them but it's rare the receiver ever knows this. But with a typed letter, from that same CEO or leader it's often assumed he/she didn't personally craft the letter.

More common today is the desire to write thank you notes by email. And this isn't just about the younger generations. Almost anyone who uses a computer tends to be more comfortable sending an email than a handwritten note. It's quicker to type a note, which is one of the main reasons it means more to the receiver when you take the time to buy stationery or correspondence cards, write out a note, stamp it and put it in the mail. Without even consciously thinking about it, they know you took time and put in more effort to say thank you than if you had sent a quick email. I've received plenty of thank you emails, and I've found that often the author doesn't even realize they are writing in the impersonal, short-phrase-and-not-complete-sentence language that is common in email exchanges. Spelling and grammatical errors are more common in emails than handwritten notes. Sending emails also runs the risk of it going to spam and never being read by the intended recipient. A potential candidate for a position in my office sent an email that I opened quickly on my iPhone while out of the office, then it disappeared and I never found a way to retrieve it. Yes, I knew she had sent me an email, but I didn't even scan it when I opened it, so I never knew what she intended to convey.

Emails also do not allow the person to savor your words long after they have been written. You can save emails or print them out, but few people ever do, and seldom look back at emails that are stored in cyberspace. On the flip side, almost everyone I know saves thank you notes that mean something to them. I have a box of thank you notes that I've saved over the years, and at least once or twice a year I read through some of them when I've had a bad day. They always remind me of the things I do well, the people who I have helped along the way, and they boost my spirits each and every time. My mother, I'm sure, is not the only one to keep her favorite notes in her Bible. When I met with executive Ben Sutton about his practice of writing thank you notes, he showed me an entire filing cabinet full of thank you notes he has received during his tenure. When I walk through the halls at work I notice that in almost every single cubicle or office employees have pinned up a note of thanks they received from someone. Handwritten notes are treasured more than emails, and if you want to convey sincere appreciation for someone, you accomplish it much more effectively by handwriting the note.

When talking with students or others who are seeking internships or employment, the question about handwritten note or email is always a hot topic. The practice of sending an email to thank an interviewer has become more popular over the years, not just because it's easy, but because it's timely. Candidates can send an email just moments after leaving an interview, and many don't want to have a handwritten note show up days after other candidates have fired off emails in hours following their visit. While I understand this concern, I still believe that the handwritten note is always the better option, even if it means you do both. I have had job candidates send me a quick email the day following their interview, and then follow it up with a handwritten note. This is perfectly acceptable and allows you to send your appreciation quickly, while following up with a more personal, thought out handwritten note of appreciation that will distinguish you from all of the other candidates who choose only email. Be prepared to send the follow-up handwritten note as soon as possible after the interview. Long before he became CEO of the Campbell Soup Company, Doug Conant, when interviewing for jobs, went to a nearby coffee shop immediately following the interview and handwrote his thank you notes to everyone he met.

With a little bit of planning and discipline, this can become an easy habit, and one that will always give you an advantage over those who rely solely on email. There will be instances when all you can do is write a thank you by email, and email thank you notes are certainly better than none at all. Still, nothing beats the impact of a handwritten note.

**TIP**

*For those who do not have elegant handwriting (and I'm one of those) or for those who think better when they are typing, take the time to compose your thank you notes while you are at the computer. Then print them out and copy them onto note cards so you can focus exclusively on your handwriting. Often before a business trip, I type out 10-15 thank you notes and pack them in my bag along with correspondence cards and stamps so I can copy them in my handwriting when I'm at a hotel or coffee shop or even on a plane.*

## You don't have to write a book

I'm a writer, so I don't mind writing long notes to people and often run out of space on note cards unless I've planned out in advance what I want to say. But my most effective notes are often the ones that are shorter. Thank you notes should be clear and concise, with a message that is simple, brief and meaningful. I've heard people say that they freeze up when they look at a blank note card, because they think they need to write paragraphs to convey how thankful they are. No one wants to read a long, drawn out note any more than you want to write one. Don't feel pressure to fill up the page. If you write more than really needs to be said, you are likely to wander off topic in your message, which can water down what you are trying to convey. A well written thank you note that is two sentences is infinitely more powerful than a page of rambling thoughts. And for those who think writing notes is too time consuming, I recommend never spending more than ten minutes on one note. Say what you want to say, and then put the pen down.

**TIP** *Buy notecards that are small so that a few sentences can fill up the page. The larger your card, the more you will feel* *compelled to fill it up even if you have nothing more to say. Buy cards that have a pattern or a dark color on the back so you won't feel as though you need to continue writing on the other side. Long notes aren't always bad, but you should always have a stock of small cards. Most notes don't require an epistle.*

## Say why it matters

In the many formulas given for writing thank you notes, being specific is always mentioned. We want to receive notes that specifically mention the gift, kindness, or favor. Otherwise, we can guess that the author is firing off multiple notes in one sitting and doesn't even really know for what he/she is thanking us. They are checking us off their list, and while it is better than nothing, it certainly doesn't make us feel appreciated.

We've all gotten these notes:

*Dear Sally,*

*Thank you so much for the gorgeous flower vase you sent for my birthday.*

*I will use it in my kitchen this summer when my garden is blooming and think of you. I look forward to seeing you again soon.*

*Thanks Again,*
*Becky*

There is nothing *wrong* with this note, but we know that the recipient is writing many of these and filling in the blanks as they go. I would be happy to receive a note like this from someone because they are, in fact, thanking me, but I would not feel that my gift was all that meaningful, and I would know the thank you was obligatory.

No matter what the circumstance is that prompts a thank you note, the recipient of the note should be able to understand why their kindness matters, how it made a difference, and what the impact was. An alternative to the note above is the following:

*Dear Sally,*

*One of my very favorite things in life is fresh flowers in my house. Every Friday when I leave work, I stop by the flower stand and pick up a new bouquet because they brighten up my house and often my mood! When I received the lovely vase you sent me for my birthday, I knew I had just the perfect place for it on my mantle. I will think of you every Friday when I put fresh flowers in it. I am grateful for our friendship and for the many ways you brighten my life! I will look forward to seeing you when you are next in town.*

*With gratitude,*
*Becky*

This note, in just a few extra sentences, conveys a much greater sense of gratitude than the other note. It adds a personal touch that shows the recipient that the gift really does have meaning and impact.

If someone gives you their time and advice, try to convey to them what that meant to you. What progress or conclusions were you able to make based on their advice? If a friend runs an errand for you in a busy week, tell them what it allowed you to accomplish in that gift of time and the peace of mind it gave you. When a colleague goes to bat for you on a project, show how the confidence they placed in you boosted your own self confidence and made you more apt to speak up in meetings. When you are able to convey the impact of what someone has done for you, the thank you is meaningful and sincere and will be remembered.

Within my department at work, we often ask scholarship recipients to write thank you notes to their donors, sometimes anonymously and sometimes by name. Every year there are notes that stand out from the rest, and they are always from the students who intuitively understand that their benefactor doesn't want to be thanked as much as they want to know that their generosity has made an impact on the student. Very often the majority of the notes will say something to the effect of:

*Dear Donor,*

*Thank you for the scholarship you provided for me this past semester.*

*I was so happy to find out I was the recipient. If it were not for your generosity, I would never be able to attend this great university. I hope I will be able to meet you in person at the scholarship brunch in October.*

*Sincerely,*
*Student*

While I'm sure the donor is happy to receive any handwritten note of thanks, most donors say they don't want to be thanked as much as they want to know that their gift has had an impact. A note that will express this impact might look something like this:

*Dear Donor,*

*Earlier this week I attended a panel discussion on campus about the role the media plays in shaping our personal political views. Afterwards a professor and I had coffee together to talk about it in more depth, and it was one of the most interesting and engaging conversations I can remember having. The professor invited me to sign up for one of his classes next semester on the media, one that is usually in high demand and closes out early. I am learning more than I ever thought possible and I am so grateful to you. Your generosity makes things like this a reality for me. I hope I can share with you more experiences like this when I meet you at the scholarship brunch in October.*

*Sincerely,*
*Student*

Sometimes focusing on impact, rather than a specific gift or kindness, is a necessity and not a choice. One day I got a call from a friend of a friend who had recently gotten married. In the chaos of the day, the thing every bride dreads happened. While transporting the wedding gifts brought by guests to the reception, her family somehow separated the cards from the gifts. When she returned from her honeymoon, she opened all of the gifts, as well as the cards, but had no idea who had given her which present. Her friend contacted me to ask what to do in a case like this. While I felt sorry for the bride, I was also secretly happy to know this would ultimately result in her wedding guests receiving more interesting and engaging notes than if she was able to match the giver with a gift.

I gave my friend some advice on what I would do if I was in the same situation. A thank you note might look something like this:

*Dear Jim and Susie,*

*Well, my almost perfect wedding fell a little short when the unthinkable happened ... our wedding gifts were separated from our cards and now we have a lot of wonderful gifts but no idea who gave us what! Greg and I so appreciate the generosity of our friends and family and since you always pick out the perfect thing for me I'm sure your gift is one of my favorites. But more than a material present, I was so happy that you could be with us on our wedding day. I remember walking down the aisle and seeing your face smiling up at me and thinking how fortunate I am to have such a great friend, willing to travel across the country during your busy season, to share in my joy. I can't imagine that day without you. Your note meant so much to me, especially the tips for a happy marriage. Greg and I will read that more than once for sure! We look forward to catching up when we are back from the honeymoon! Maybe then you can tell me which present was yours!*

*Love,*
*Stacey*

I'm sure that many of the bride's friends got a laugh out of her notes, and the situation allowed the bride to focus on her relationships and their meaning to her, which likely had a greater impact on her friends and relatives. In almost any situation where you are writing a thank you note for a gift, spend a little time on the gift and its impact, but then try to focus on the person who gave the gift, and what that person means to you.

**TIP**

*Try writing notes without using the words "thank you." While difficult at first, you will find that it forces you to be more creative and interesting. "Thank you" is often a crutch in notes that can make the note feel like a carbon copy of every other note someone receives. At the very least, avoid using it in the first line of your note. Instead of saying "Dear Laine, thank you so much for spending time at the winery with me on my birthday," try saying "Dear Laine, I can't think of a better way to spend my birthday than in the company of great friends and great wine."*

If you are writing to thank someone for their advice or a conversation you had with them, try to quote something they said to you and how it impacted your thinking. This is always an ego boost to the recipient and it shows that you really did pay attention to what they were saying. It also shows that it was helpful advice, which is what they really want to know. The graduating senior who wrote me a note to thank me for my career advice used this technique and it was a perfect way to show his gratitude:

*I feel like seeing you this morning was a God-sent gift during this particularly hard decision-making time. Just talking to you helped me make my decision, in particular when you said "you can't make a wrong decision." With this in mind, I had the freedom to continue to process my options and came to a resolution to take the admissions job. I'm sure you weren't anticipating that you would help me so much but you did and I want to thank you for that.*

**TIP**

*Sometimes it makes sense to write more than one thank you note. When I receive gift certificates, I usually write a quick and simple note so the person knows I received it, and then once I use the certificate, I write another one that might say, in part, "This week was one of the craziest weeks I've had in a while and the only thing that kept me going was knowing that there was a massage waiting for me at the end of it. What a great way to relax and unwind!"*

*I also do this when I can't remember (gasp!) if I ever wrote the original note of thanks. This covers my bases. Writing a note long after the kindness is also help-ful with advice that you find yourself using even months or years after it was given, or a gift that continues to bring you joy into the future.*

## Show Your Personality

In many cases, your notes will be much more interesting, engaging and meaningful if you make them personal to who you are. Don't be afraid to show some personality, and even humor, in your notes. It's a lot more fun to write AND to read these notes, and they are usually the ones that stand out among all of the standard thank you notes that say very little other than thank you.

I love quotes, so often I will include a favorite quote that is relevant to the gift, friend, or occa-sion. And if I don't have one that fits, sometimes I put in one that I've always loved:

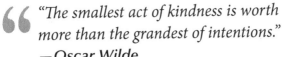 *"The smallest act of kindness is worth more than the grandest of intentions."*
—Oscar Wilde

A friend of mine is an artist, and she is great at drawing scenes, cartoons, or funny characters. I always love getting her notes because I know there will be something fun and funny to look at in addition to reading her words. A few years ago I visited some friends of my parents in England, and I took some pictures of their house at sunset while I was there. I printed them out and included them with my thank you note. She emailed me later to say that she so enjoyed receiving the pictures that showed her house in a way she hadn't really seen it before, and she loved being reminded how much she loves her home.

I love notes that are humorous when it's appropriate, and this works not just in personal notes but in professional notes as well. In the past few years I've received two notes that continue to make me smile, and laugh, whenever I re-read them or think about them.

This was from an alumna who had attended a gala. I sometimes get voice mails like this from her as well, but having it in writing was a real treat!

*Your fete on Friday evening was wonderful – the food outstanding. The service was seamless and invisible and perhaps just too much wine. All in all, a perfectly executed evening for a very congenial group. Thank you for your superior planning – it showed. As an invited guest, I feel that this was not an ordinary event by any stretch of the imagination. Here is what I would like to know:*

1) *Can you handle a dinner party of 6 or must it always be 500?*
2) *Do you go home and eat Special K, obsess over what did not go well, and throw objects across the room at imaginary people who bossed you around or made you upset? I want to know. The National Enquirer wants to know! You are amazing and lovely in every way.*

The next, and perhaps my all-time favorite, came from a trustee, who handwrote it on his iPad, scanned and emailed it to me the morning

69

after a major event. It's a testament to the fact that a note can be extremely brief and still have great impact. This is the note in its entirety:

Dear Jennifer,

Thank you for last night. I am convinced that if you had planned D-Day, the Germans would have abandoned their positions without a shot being fired. Last night was magic.

Jim

**TIP**

*Notes are always more interesting and fun if they include something besides the note – a picture of the gift itself and where it's being used, a picture of you with the recipient, a book of matches or cardboard coaster from a restaurant where you spent a fun night with a friend. This can also be effective in professional situations, usually with an article that is relevant to a conversation you have had with the recipient or an interesting study that relates to the job for which you are applying. I read a ton of articles, and often they remind me of someone specific and a conversation we've had in the past. While it's tempting to forward links to articles in an email, I usually print them out and use it as an opportunity to write a thank you note.*

*A few years ago I read an article on the ten major mistakes bosses make. I sent it to my first boss and told her how glad I was that my first job experience was so positive and that it was in large part due to her, someone who had never made any mistakes listed in the article.*

## Anonymous Thank You Notes are Magic

Recently a friend of mine was called in to his manager's office. He wanted to talk with him about something that had been brought to his attention by another colleague. My friend had written something on Facebook that the colleague thought put their organization in a negative light, and instead of telling my friend directly, the colleague went to their manager. The manager insisted on protecting the identity of this person, so my friend never knew who had said this about him. For weeks, even months, he wondered who had gone behind his back. In meetings he looked around the room at the faces and wondered who might have been the one to turn him in to the manager. Without any direct knowledge of whom it might be, he suspected everyone, and it began to affect his relationships with his colleagues because he didn't know whom to trust. So he trusted no one, and it made his work infinitely more difficult.

The beauty of an anonymous thank you note is that it has the same effect, but in a positive way. When you receive a note praising you for something you did and it isn't signed, you will begin to imagine that anyone, and in fact *everyone*, around you could have written it. And instead of distrusting everyone, like my friend, you will begin to see positive possibilities in everyone. It's magic ... pure magic.

Earlier I mentioned a note that a student had written to me during a particularly bad week, a note that was left under my office door in the middle of the night. What I didn't mention is the note was anonymous. In fact, it was signed "on behalf of all Wake Forest Students." Had the note been signed by a particular student, I would not have loved the note any less, and in fact I would have reached out to the student so I could tell him or her just how much it meant to me and lifted my spirits. But because it was anonymous, I saw potential in every student's face I passed in the halls or on the Quad. I had inexplicably good feelings about every student, because I saw every one of them as the potential author.

After receiving this note, I was determined to try it out for myself. Later that semester I attended a meeting that was pretty intense. Emotions were high and decisions needed to be made but there were some underlying issues that everyone knew about, but no one wanted to bring to the table for fear of upsetting the senior level managers. Towards the end of the meeting, one of the more reserved members of the group asked to say some things. She then calmly and professionally brought the issues to the forefront, and we ended up making wise and effective decisions that might not have been made without her input. After the meeting, I decided to write her a note of thanks, and I told her how courageous I thought she was, and how appreciative I was that someone in the room was willing to say what many of us were thinking but not prepared to articulate. I told her that she changed the trajectory and outcome of the meeting in a positive way that was in line with our core values and our mission as a department. And then I decided not to sign it. Not because I was scared or ashamed to attach my name to it, but because I knew it would mean more to her if it was possible that it came from anyone in the room, even a member of senior management. I love thinking about her reaction when she read the note, and the wonder she must have had for weeks on end about who could have written it.

**TIP**

*Secret Santa has been around for years, and there is a reason for that. People love mystery, and they love believing that kindness can come from anywhere, even the most unexpected of places. Find reasons to send anonymous notes ... you aren't likely to see the outcome of your note, but you can enjoy thinking about the positive effect it will have on the recipient.*

## It is NEVER too late!

It's always good to be timely with your thank you notes, and in most situations I try to write and mail them as soon as I can. But there are times when a belated thank you note is very effective, and even more meaningful if it's written long after the gift or kindness has been received. I've never, in all of my conversations about thank you notes, had someone complain about a late thank you note, even if it appeared years later. Most people are flattered that someone remembered a kindness so long after it occurred.

In one of my sessions with entering freshmen at Wake Forest, I encouraged them to think about people who had helped them get where they are today, and then I asked them to write five thank you notes to people to thank them for what they had done. One student said that three years earlier when she was on her first college tour she stayed with a friend of her mother's, and the friend had given her some good advice about her college search, but she had never written her a note. "It seems strange to write it now," she said, "and I'm embarrassed I never wrote it before now." I told her to say just that in her note ... to say that she was so sorry she had never written but that now that she was entering her freshman year she had been thinking a lot about her visit three years ago and how helpful the advice had been in her search for just the right college. I'm guessing her mother's friend was delighted to receive the note and to hear just how helpful she had been.

My favorite stories always come from people who choose to write someone from their past. I encourage this in my talks, in large part because I think these notes really are the most powerful. When coaches and teachers and relatives and first bosses receive notes from someone they helped long ago, telling them that they made a positive impact on someone's life, it can be incredibly validating and affirming. As with the counselor I wrote months after I had moved away, my note landed in his box when he needed most to hear those words. We never know when someone may need to hear words of affirmation, so writing them long after the fact may be just the right time.

During my first year out of college, one of my favorite high school teachers was diagnosed with cancer. I was traveling that entire year with a training program, and I wasn't able to go home to visit her, even though we knew that her illness was terminal. Over and over I would tell myself that I needed to write her a note to tell her I was thinking about her, but also to thank her for all that I had learned from her. I kept putting it off for all the reasons you can think of ... not enough time, no cards or stamps, not sure what to say, etc., etc. Finally, after a few weeks of stalling, I sat down in a coffee shop to compose my note. A note that I knew, essentially, was my goodbye note to her. I told her that her world history class made me care of things greater than myself, and that as a selfish teenager who had hated history up to that point, she showed me that history was a series of stories, with outcomes good and bad, that we could learn from if we paid attention. And for a sheltered child who up to that point had never gone outside the southeast, her world geography class transported me to places I never dreamed I would go in my own lifetime. She instilled in me a love for travel that I have to this day, and she even helped me win the geography category every time in Trivial Pursuit. After shedding a few tears, I sealed the envelope, stamped it and put it in the mail. Two days later my mother called to let me know that Mrs. Jolly had passed away. I was devastated by her death, but also sad because I knew she had not received my letter in time. Sometimes, late really can be too late.

The bright side of this story is that the letter arrived the day that Mrs. Jolly died, and her sons and daughter read the letter. They told my mother that they were touched by my words, and that I had captured the essence of who she was as a teacher, and they asked if they could read some of my letter at her memorial service. I was unable to be at that service, but I was there in spirit, and I was honored that my words were read. I know now that Mrs. Jolly heard them. So it was a good ending to a time of real anguish for me that I had not written my thank you to her earlier, and a good reminder that we should never wait to tell someone they are appreciated.

**TIP**

*Keep a list of people who have been special in your life or who have impacted your life in a positive way. Make it a habit once a week, or even once a month, to write to someone on your list. The impact you will have on those people will be immeasurable.*

# Good Habits Die Hard – Making a Difference One Thank You Note at a Time

Note writing will never become a habit, much less an easy habit, if we constantly put roadblocks in the way. There are a number of simple, easy and quick steps you can take to make writing notes a part of your weekly or even daily routine. I've followed these for years and it has made notes a habit for me in a way that is often fun and takes up an amazingly small amount of time in a very busy schedule. If you do a little bit of work on the front end, writing notes will become something that is second nature.

## Stay stocked!

Many notes never get written simply because notecards, or pens, or stamps aren't close by.

It's amazing how many more notes I write when I am fully stocked with these items and keep them in plain view, with easy access. I keep notecards, pens and stamps at work and at home, so I can write notes whenever I have free time. In my previous job, my team had a basket of notes that was kept in a common area where we could all see and access them at any time. In the basket was a variety of cards – plain, simple, flowery, masculine, large, small, and everything else in between. We kept this well stocked all the time so that having the right materials was never an excuse not to write a note. I also kept notecards and stamps on my desk so that even when I was feeling incredibly lazy, I didn't have to walk to the basket but could reach over and pull out a variety of notecards at any point.

I don't live close to a post office, and even the one I use on a fairly regular basis has a nightmare of a parking lot, so I don't rely on a trip to the post office to get my stamps. I order them online, have them shipped to my office or home, and always make sure to re-order before I run out. I've have plenty of friends and colleagues who, over the years, have written countless thank you notes that never got mailed because they didn't have stamps, and after a few weeks of sitting on a desk or a counter, they threw it away because they didn't think it was timely anymore. Don't let this be an excuse for someone missing out on receiving your words of gratitude.

## Go mobile

I travel with cards and stamps and a variety of pens so that I can write notes on a moment's notice when I have a reason to be thankful. As I mentioned before, it's common for me to type out a series of thank you notes and then copy them by hand while I'm on the road. But I also write notes to those I meet, people who greet me or serve me or do something nice for me. Often if a member of the hotel staff is especially kind or goes out of their way for me, I will write a note and leave it for them at the front desk when I check out. When I'm a houseguest, it's not uncommon for me to leave a note for the host on the dresser or bed when I leave. I find that if I write the notes right then and there, they get written 100% of the time. If I wait until I return home to write the notes, there's a good chance that something else takes my attention or time and it's easier to let it slide. Always travel with a stock of cards and stamps and try to write notes as soon as you can, even on the road, while you are sitting in an airport or waiting for a meeting to begin. Something this simple can greatly increase the number of thank you notes you send.

## Be creative with your materials

Often it only takes a sentence or two to let a person know that you're grateful for something they have done. So you don't need a full notecard and if you use a big card in these situations there is too much white space and you will feel compelled to fill it up. To alleviate this issue, keep postcards on hand and use them for mini-notes of thanks. Travel postcards, funny postcards, anything that is appropriate for the situation. I love the postcards that are black and white photos from the '50s and '60s. They always make me laugh and I modify them to suit my purposes. Before a road trip with a friend, I sent her one of these postcards with a woman lying on a chaise lounge smoking a cigarette and the words above her head said "I feel a sin coming on." I wrote to my friend how much I was looking forward to our weekend and how grateful I was for her friendship and upcoming adventure.

Birthday cards or other greeting cards are another great source for thank you notes. When you receive a card in the mail and the sender didn't write on the left inside panel, tear the card in half and turn the card into a postcard that you can send as a thank you. Quite often the front of the card is perfect for a postcard. At any given time, I have a stack of these postcards and it makes it incredibly easy to shoot off a quick thank you note to someone. There's no rule that you have to send a thank you on stationery, or card stock, or in an envelope. Some of the best responses I've received from thank you notes I've written are those that were on postcards or other unexpected material.

## Steal ideas from others

Some people have a knack for saying thank you in just the right way, and I love receiving these notes. I also love stealing (ahem ... borrowing) their ideas or phrases. If you don't save every note you receive, at least save the best ones, or the ones that really made you laugh (or cry) and refer to them when you are stumped on how to express your gratitude. You can copy a key phrase or even a great opening to a thank you note and use it as your own. I won't tell anyone.

## Steal from yourself

Inevitably, you will write notes that make you proud. And when you do, you should make a copy of the note and use it again and again and again.

While every note I write is personal to the recipient, I do often repeat phrases or ways to say thank you (without using those words) because they work. And when they work, you should use them! Don't try to make every single note completely unique. It will drive you crazy and is completely unnecessary.

## Practice, practice, practice!

In Kralik's book, his final piece of advice about writing thank you notes is to "write a lot of them." He noted that as he came to the latter part of the year when he had written more notes than he ever had before in his life, he "got directly to the heart of what I wanted to say to my correspondents, and showed that I could sincerely appreciate and understand them and their efforts."

The best way to make writing thank you notes an easy habit is simple ... write as many as you can, as often as you can. The more you write, the easier they get. Because I've written so many notes over the years, they really do come as second nature to me. I don't spend time agonizing over just the right thing to say anymore ... it just comes naturally and easily. The same will happen to you if you JUST KEEP WRITING.

## MAKE IT MATTER

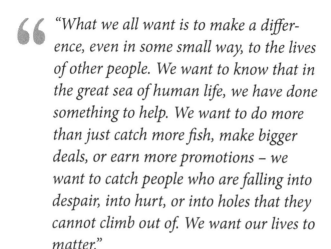 *"What we all want is to make a difference, even in some small way, to the lives of other people. We want to know that in the great sea of human life, we have done something to help. We want to do more than just catch more fish, make bigger deals, or earn more promotions – we want to catch people who are falling into despair, into hurt, or into holes that they cannot climb out of. We want our lives to matter."*
—*M. Craig Barnes*

Last month, a friend called me from two time zones away to tell me that he had had the best day he could remember in a really long time, all because he received a note from someone thanking him for just being ... him. The author told my friend that there were many lives that were better, and richer, and more joyful, because of him. My friend was emotional as he told me that if he never received another thank you note in his hopefully very long life, this was enough. And because he knew how much I would love this story, he called me right away.

I decided a long time ago that my contribution to the world was likely never going to be through grand or monumental deeds and accomplishments. But like most people, I want my life to make a difference. I want to know that I've left the world a little better than I found it. And writing notes of gratitude, I believe, is one very special way to make a difference. It has the power to change moods, attitudes, relationships, LIVES. Thank you notes are powerful in ways we can never fully understand or imagine. And they cost us almost nothing.

As Princeton Theological Seminary President Craig Barnes says in the quote above, we want our lives to matter. And when other people matter to you, in small and large and unexpected ways, you should let them know. Write those words that can make all the difference in the world to them.

They deserve it.

You deserve it.

And the world will be just a little bit better because of it.

# About the Author

Jennifer Richwine has written thousands of thank you notes (and received her fair share) throughout the last twenty-one years of her professional career in sales, conference planning, marketing and admissions for a girls' boarding school, and planning and executing the  signature events for Wake Forest University. Her reputation for writing memorable and timely thank you notes over the years led to her development of her talk "The Art and the Power of the Thank You Note" that she has given to various groups at universities, churches and professional organizations.

However, she is even more touched by the personal thank you notes she has written and received over the years. She hopes to bring the power of the thank you to others, reinforce the importance for those already in the habit, and make it easy for those procrastinators out there to take the first step and express their gratitude to those around them.

Jennifer currently is the Executive Director of the Washington D.C. Office for Wake Forest University. You might spot her on a Saturday morning at a local coffee shop in our nation's capital, writing out one of her many thank you notes.

Made in the USA
Middletown, DE
31 January 2015